LITERACY TECHNIQUES:
FOR TEACHERS AND PARENTS
(Third Edition)

Peter Edwards

KH

Marcus E. Spicer did the artwork in this book.
Susan, Dean and Monique Edwards contributed additional work.

Printed in Victoria, Canada

National Library of Canada Cataloguing in Publication Data

Edwards, Peter
        Literacy techniques for teachers and parents / written by Peter Edwards. -- 3rd ed.
ISBN 1-4120-0746-1
        I. Title.
LC149.E38 2003   372.6   C2003-903883-1

TRAFFORD

This book was published on-demand in cooperation with Trafford Publishing.
On-demand publishing is a unique process and service of making a book available for retail
sale to the public taking advantage of on-demand manufacturing and Internet marketing.
On-demand publishing includes promotions, retail sales, manufacturing, order fulfilment, accounting and collecting royalties on behalf of the author.

Suite 6E, 2333 Government St., Victoria, B.C. V8T 4P4, CANADA
Phone   250-383-6864   Toll-free   1-888-232-4444 (Canada & US)
Fax   250-383-6804   E-mail   sales@trafford.com
Web site   www.trafford.com   TRAFFORD PUBLISHING IS A DIVISION OF TRAFFORD HOLDINGS LTD.
Trafford Catalogue #03-1114   www.trafford.com/robots/03-1114.html

10   9   8   7   6   5   4   3   2

11/22/04

Contents

PREFACE TO THIRD EDITION

The major goal of the third edition of *Literacy Techniques* continues to provide educators, parents and caregivers with a number of successful, instructional techniques to assist learners to improve their literacy. Many students who are experiencing literacy problems today are in need of carefully planned and structured learning experiences that offer the learner a wide range of creative responses. *Literacy Techniques* is designed to meet this need.

The third edition features improved graphics that illustrate and explain many of the literacy techniques and samples of students' work have been included to show the use of the techniques in the classroom.

Most of the techniques can be modified to suit any grade level from primary through high school. Educators, parents and caregivers using the book are encouraged to develop their own examples for the 50 techniques from the vast array of literature and content area material available for instruction today.

Other changes in the third edition include minor rewrites and additions to some of the techniques for greater clarification and ease of use.

The references in the bibliography have been updated to provide current literature and research dealing with the many aspects of literacy and also to encourage further reading.

The section on computer web sites has been increased to give educators access to the enormous amount of instructional materials and strategies that are now available. This latter section will continue to expand as new sites are developed and evaluated in the future.

INTRODUCTION

The definition of literacy in *Literacy Techniques: For Teachers and Parents* includes all of the language arts: reading, writing, listening and speaking, plus thinking. These skills are combined in dynamic interrelationships in the context of authentic learning experiences.

The main aim of the book is to present 50 key literacy techniques for instructional purposes, in outline and graphic form that preserve the essential elements of each technique. Although this approach lacks a detailed analysis and discussion of the techniques, these aspects are readily available in the textbooks listed in the bibliography and currently used in the field. Individuals who find that they need additional information concerning the techniques are urged to pursue the numerous source materials in the book.

Literacy Techniques is designed to assist literacy instruction in four main ways:

1. The 50 literacy techniques represent a major 'knowledge base' for individuals who need to develop effective teaching techniques in literacy.

2. The 50 literacy techniques have been carefully selected from a wide range of resources in the field. Most of the techniques are not available in a single publication.

3. The 50 literacy techniques act as an up-date for individuals who are not currently aware of the latest instructional developments in the field.

4. The over 50 web sites provide access to an enormous amount of literacy resources that can be used in the classroom and in the home.

A major benefit of using the book is that it provides summaries of literacy techniques that can be quickly applied to a variety of learning situations. The book can be used by undergraduate and graduate candidates, by pre-service and practicing teachers, as well as other caregivers involved in home schooling, family literacy, or working as literacy volunteers. The techniques enable them to use interesting and valuable activities to strengthen and encourage their students to achieve their full learning potential.

The literacy techniques are not intended for use solely with remedial readers. They include ideas suitable for use with primary, elementary, middle and high school students, as well as with students requiring special assistance or acceleration in their programs. A wide variety of hands-on activities, including the use of computer programs, is a natural follow-up to most of the techniques included in *Literacy Techniques: For Teachers and Parents*.

The 50 literacy techniques deal with **word analysis, sight words, vocabulary development, literal** and **non-literal comprehension, fluency and rate, writing skills, study skills, metacognition, metalanguage** and **motivation**. Each technique includes a reference source, a brief description, suggested instructional levels, a step-by-step procedure (often with examples), and in many cases a graphic that illustrates major aspects of the technique. Many of the techniques presented in this book offer ways to develop and encourage the use of **metacognition** and **metalanguage**.

Metacognition is the ability to think about our thinking and to be able to make necessary adjustments so that we can think more effectively and therefore comprehend and learn. Readers who use metacognition are able to analyze a situation, decide what skills or strategies are needed to gain understanding and then apply those skills to achieve success (Burns, Roe & Ross, 1992; Leu & Kinzer, 1995; Searfoss & Readence, 1994).

Metalanguage, or the ability to think about the words we use, is another vitally important skill that is needed in reading and writing (Durkin, 1993). **Metalinguistic awareness** usually progresses from an understanding of the sounds of the language (phonology), to an awareness of the structure or grammar of the language (syntax), to a final understanding of the meaning of the words (semantics). (Burns, Roe & Ross, 1996).

A good way to use the book is to identify the area of reading, literacy or language instruction that is needed and then locate the specific technique that is required. For ease of use, the techniques have been classified according to suggested skill areas as shown in the following chart of *Instructional Literacy Techniques*.

The abbreviations used in the chart are as follows:

P Primary School

E Elementary School

M Middle School

HS High School

R Remedial

Instructional Literacy Techniques

Technique	Level	Word Analysis	Vocabulary	Comprehension	Rate	Oral Reading	Writing	Study Skills	Metacognition
ALERT	E-M-HS			X					
ANALYTICAL PHONICS	P-E-R	X							
AUTHOR'S CHAIR	P-E					X	X		
BIG BOOKS	P-R		X	X	X	X			
CIRCLE STORIES	P-E			X					
CLOZE TECHNIQUE	E-M-HS		X	X					
CONCEPT CARDS	E-M-HS		X	X				X	
CSSR	E-M-HS		X						
DETAILS	E-M-HS		X	X				X	
DLTA	ALL		X	X					
DRA	P-E-M		X	X					
DRTA	ALL		X	X					
ECHO READING	P-E-R				X				
EXPERIENCE-TEXT-RELATIONSHIP	E-M		X	X					
GIVE ME SPACE!	P-E-M	X				X			
GUIDED IMAGERY	P-E-M			X					

Technique	Level	Word Analysis	Vocabulary	Comprehension	Rate	Oral Reading	Writing	Study Skills	Metacognition
HERRINGBONE	E-M-HS			X				X	
IMPRESS METHOD	BEGINNING								
INQUEST	HS			X	X	X			
JIFFY TECHNIQUE	P-E		X	X			X		
JOURNALS	E-M-HS			X			X		
KWL	E-M			X					X
LEA	P-E-M		X	X		X			
MAIN IDEA	E-M-HS			X				X	
MAZE	E-M		X	X					
PANORAMA	M-HS			X	X		X	X	
PHONOGRAM METHOD	P-E-R	X	X						
PICTORIAL OUTLINES	E-M-HS		X					X	
QAR	E-M			X					
READER'S THEATER	E-M					X	X		
READING LOGS	E-M-HS			X					X
REBUS WRITING	P-E-R		X	X			X		
REPEATED READINGS	GENERAL				X				
REQUEST (RECIPROCAL READING)	E-M			X		X			
SCAFFOLDING	BEGINNING		X	X					
SCHEMA THEORY	E-M-HS		X	X			X	X	

Technique	Level	Word Analysis	Vocabulary	Comprehension	Rate	Oral Reading	Writing	Study Skills	Metacognition
SCRAMBLED STORIES	P-E-M			X		X			
SFA	E-M-HS		X						
SIMILIES	E-M		X	X					
SQ3R	M-HS			X				X	
STORY FRAMES	P-E-R			X			X		
STORY GRAPHS	E-M-HS			X			X		
STORY MAPS	P-E			X			X		
STORY MOBILES	P-E-M		X	X		X			
SSR	ALL				X				
SYNTHETIC PHONICS	BEGINNING	X	X						
VAKT	BEGINNING	X	X						
VSS	SEC.		X						
VOICE POINTING	P-R		X			X			
WANTED POSTERS	E-M			X			X		

TITLE: <u>ALERT</u>

REFERENCE: Allen, E.G., Wright, J.P., & Laminack, L.L. (1988). Using language experience to ALERT pupils' critical thinking skills. <u>The Reading Teacher, 41</u>, 904-910.

INSTRUCTIONAL LEVELS: Elementary-Middle-High School

DESCRIPTION: Designed to assist students in critical reading and analysis of commercial materials and propaganda.

PROCEDURE:

1. **A - Advance Organizer.** Students are told to read materials such as advertisements to find the product or message being promoted, biased language, and any special effects used such as illustrations or endorsements by popular characters.

2. **L - Listen/Learn.** The students read the material.

3. **E - Examine/Explain.** Students evaluate the materials with the help (if needed) of teacher questions such as, "Do you think you are being persuaded to do something?"

4. **R - Restate/Read.** The students restate the meaning of the material in their own words, either independently or as a group. Information such as the title or name of the material or product, key words or phrases, and the claims of the writer can be recorded in a notebook or on a chalkboard.

5. **T - Think/Test/Talk.** Students evaluate the claims of the product or materials by testing the claims against their critical analysis.

TITLE: <u>Analytic Phonics</u>

REFERENCE: Bloomfield, L. & Barnhart, C. (1961). <u>Let's read.</u> New York: Rinehart & Winston.

INSTRUCTIONAL LEVELS: Beginning Reading

DESCRIPTION: Selected sight words are taught first and then the sounds (phonemes) of the letters or letter combinations (graphemes) within the words.

PROCEDURE:

1. Select words that contain a sound that needs to be developed; e.g. select *ship, shop, shut, dash, flash to* teach the *sh* digraph.

2. Teach the whole word first, concentrating on each sound in the word.

3. Practice saying the word.

4. Teach the sounds of the letters and word parts.

5. Practice writing the word.

6. Place the word in context.

7. Use the word in context.

Example: Teach the digraph *sh*. Select the word *ship.*

Analyze ship= sh (digraph) -i (short vowel) *p (consonant).*

Say each part. Write the word: *ship*

Sentence work; "I saw a big *ship* ".

Practice: Use the word *ship in* activities.

Extension Work: Use other words containing the digraph *sh* (e.g. *shop, shut) in* a similar manner.

TITLE: Author's Chair

REFERENCE: Graves, D.H., & Hansen, J. (1983). The author's chair. Language Arts, 53, 645-651.

INSTRUCTIONAL LEVELS: Primary-Elementary

DESCRIPTION: A special chair is placed in the classroom where children can read their creative, written work to the other members of the class and be recognized as authors.

PROCEDURE:

1.   The classroom has a special chair designated as an "Author's Chair".

2.   Children sit in the chair and read their work to the rest of the class.

3.   Children who are reading their creative work begin to realize that they are authors.

4.   Children's creative work can be made into books and placed in the classroom and/or the school library.

5.   The books should include an "All About the Author" page with a photograph of the child.

TITLE: Big Books

REFERENCE: Holdaway, D. (1979). The foundations of literacy.
                  New York: Ashton Scholastic.

INSTRUCTIONAL LEVELS: Primary-Remedial

DESCRIPTION: A shared book activity where repetitive and

predictable stories are read to children using an oversize book with

large illustrations.

PROCEDURE:

Step 1.   Look at the cover of the book and predict what the story may
           be about.

Step 2.   Stress the fact that it is a real story aspect, written by
           an author and illustrated by an artist.

Step 3.   Look at the pictures and the print on the title page of the book
           and predict other things about the story.

Step 4.   Read the title together.

Step 5.   Read the story together.

Step 6.   Use your hand to guide the children's reading.

Step 7.   Stop reading and predict what may happen next.

Step 8.   Read to verify what did happen in the story.

Step 9.   Look at the back cover and take note of the pictures and
           symbols that tell about the end of the story.

Step 10.   Develop follow-up activities based on the story in the book.

TITLE: <u>Circle Stories</u>

REFERENCE: Jett-Simpson, M. (1981). Writing stories using

model structures: The circle story. <u>Language Arts</u>, <u>58,</u>

293-230.

INSTRUCTIONAL LEVELS: Primary-Elementary

DESCRIPTION: Developing comprehension through the use of repetitive stories
or content-area materials that have a sequence of events that begin and end at the
same point.

PROCEDURE:

1.   Select a story where the character or characters begin at a starting point
and finish up at the same place at the end of the story.

2.   Divide a large circle into the number of events or incidents that there are in
the story and number these pie shapes clockwise (see following diagram).

3.   Read the story to the children, discuss the sequence of events, and let them
decide where to write or draw each of the events on the circle.

4.   Discuss the cause and effect of each event or incident in the story.

5.   Practice repeated readings of the story with individuals or groups of
children.

6.   Use the circle story idea in other content areas to teach children the
        seasons (social studies), the life cycle of an insect or the water cycle
(science), or the months of the year (math).

Circle Stories

Note cause and effect between events.

The circle should have similar beginning and end points.

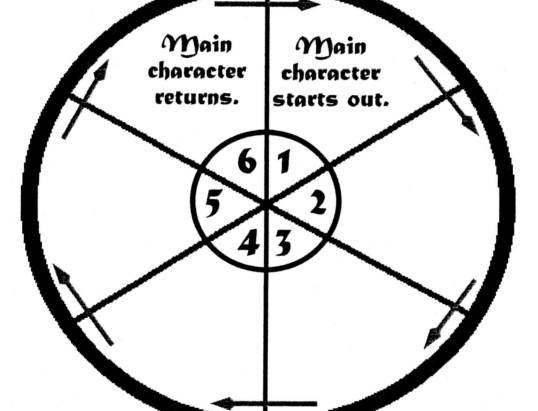

Main character returns.

Main character starts out.

6 1
5 2
4 3

Divide the circle into a number of adventures which vary with each story.

Pictures or sentences can represent events.

Circle Story

Source: <u>The Runaway Bunny</u>, by Margaret Wise Brown.

TITLE: <u>Cloze Technique</u>

REFERENCE: Taylor, W. (1953). Cloze procedure: A new tool for measuring readability. <u>Journalism Quarterly, 30,</u> 415-433.

INSTRUCTIONAL LEVELS: Elementary-Middle-High School DESCRIPTION:

A technique where readers fill in blank spaces with the correct words to make sense of a passage of prose. Cloze can be used to measure a person's reading level; to determine the readability of a reading selection; or as an instructional device to teach reading and language.

PROCEDURE:

1. Before giving a cloze test, demonstrate how the cloze technique works on the board with sample sentences.

2. Select a reading passage of approximately 275 words (or shorter for younger children) from material that has not been presented in class.

3. Leave the first sentence intact. (For younger children, leave a paragraph). Starting with the next sentence, select at random one of the first five words and delete it (For younger children, delete every seventh word). Type the sentence and leave an underlined blank of 10 spaces under the deleted word.

4. Delete every fifth word thereafter (every seventh word for younger children), until there is a total of 50 underlined blanks. (Use 20 blanks for younger children). Finish the last sentence that has a word deleted . Type one more sentence intact. (For younger children, leave a paragraph).

5. Students are not to use their textbooks in completing the cloze exercise.

6. Count as correct every <u>exact word</u> students supply.

7. Use the following reading evaluation scale: Independent = 60% correct; Instructional = 40% correct; Frustrated = below 40% correct.

Cloze Exercise (Fifth word deletions)

Weather and Climate

The atmosphere is the envelope of air that surrounds the Earth. The condition of the _____ levels of the atmosphere _____ a locality at any is of great importance _____ all forms of plant, _____ and human life.

Weather _____ the state of the _____ at a certain place _____ a certain time. Weather, _____ , refers to how hot _____ is and if it _____ dry or wet, calm _____ windy. A feature of _____ in most parts of world is that it _____ from day to day, _____ from hour to hour.

_____ over a long period _____ years, any place is _____ to have a typical _____ of weather that can _____ expected from month to and from season to _____ . The pattern is the _____ of the place. Climate _____ a most important principle _____ geography as it helps _____ to understand the conditions _____ which people live in areas of the Earth's _____ . For example some parts _____ the world are hot _____ through the year and _____ a heavy rainfall in _____ month. Since these places _____ all close to the _____ they are said to an Equatorial climate. Certain _____ parts of the world _____ warm, dry summers and _____ _____ , wet winters. Many places _____ the Mediterranean Sea have _____ type of climate that _____ therefore known as the _____ climate.

As soon as _____ know that a place _____ a particular type of there are certain things _____ can predict. We can _____ , for instance, whether the _____ vegetation is likely to be forest, grass or scrub. This in turn indicates whether such human activities as timber milling, the herding of sheep or cattle, farming or fruit growing are possible there.

Cloze Answers (Fifth word deletions)

Weather and Climate

The atmosphere is the envelope of air that surrounds the Earth. The condition of the **lower** levels of the atmosphere **over** a locality at any **time** is of great importance **to** all forms of plant, **animal** and human life.

Weather **is** the state of the **atmosphere** at a certain place **and** a certain time. Weather, **therefore**, refers to how hot **it** is and if it **is** dry or wet, calm **or** windy. A feature of **weather** in most parts of **the** world is that it **changes** from day to day, **sometimes** from hour to hour.

Taken over a long period **of** years, any place is **found** to have a typical **pattern** of weather that can **be** expected from month to **month** and from season to **season**. The pattern is the **climate** of the place. Climate **is** a most important principle **in** geography as it helps **us** to understand the conditions **under** which people live in **different** areas of the Earth's **surface**. For example some parts **of** the world are hot **all** through the year and **have** a heavy rainfall in **every** month. Since these places **are** all close to the **equator** they are said to **have** an Equatorial climate. Certain **other** parts of the world **have** warm, dry summers and **mild,** wet winters. Many places **around** the Mediterranean Sea have **this** type of climate that **is** therefore known as the **Mediterranean** climate.

As soon as **we** know that a place **has** a particular type of **climate** there are certain things **we** can predict. We can **tell**, for instance, whether the **natural** vegetation is likely to be forest, grass or scrub. This in turn indicates whether such human activities as timber milling, the herding of sheep or cattle, farming or fruit growing are possible there.

Cloze Exercise (Seventh word deletions)

The Bunyip

Ken Kangaroo lived in the Australian bush. (*Bush* is an Australian word for *forest*). Ken was happy with his friends Kathy Koala, Peter Platypus and Emily Emu. All day they would sit under a tree and talk or play games.

One day while the animals were _____ under a tree, Wendy Wombat came _____ visit them. Wendy lived on the _____ side of the bush and she _____ them a strange story. This is _____ she told them.

"In another part _____ the bush, far away, a big _____ was scaring the animals. The monster _____ called Bunyip. It lived in a _____ billabong that is an Australian word _____ swamp. At night, when it was _____, Bunyip would come out of the _____ and make loud noises. None of _____ animals could sleep, except for Ollie _____, who slept during the day. The _____ were scared and didn't know what _____ do. Would Ken and his friends _____ and help them?"

Wendy Wombat ended _____ story and looked at the friends. _____ Kangaroo looked at Kathy Koala. Kathy _____ at Peter Platypus. Peter looked at Emily Emu.

Then they all looked at Wendy Wombat. They smiled and they nodded their heads. Yes, the friends would all go and help the other animals!

Cloze Answers (Seventh word answers)

The Bunyip

Ken Kangaroo lived in the Australian bush. (*Bush* is an Australian word for *forest*). Ken was happy with his friends Kathy Koala, Peter Platypus and Emily Emu. All day they would sit under a tree and talk or play games.

One day while the animals were **resting** under a tree, Wendy Wombat came **to** visit them. Wendy lived on the **other** side of the bush and she **told** them a strange story. This is **what** she told them.
"In another part **of** the bush, far away, a big **monster** was scaring the animals. The monster **was** called Bunyip. It lived in a **large** billabong that is an Australian word **for** swamp. At night, when it was **dark,** Bunyip would come out of the **billabong** and make loud noises. None of **the** animals could sleep, except for Ollie **Owl**, who slept during the day. The **animals** were scared and didn't know what **to** do. Would Ken and his friends **come** and help them?"

Wendy Wombat ended **her** story and looked at the friends.
Ken Kangaroo looked at Kathy Koala. Kathy **looked** at Peter Platypus.
Peter looked at Emily Emu.

Then they all looked at Wendy Wombat. They smiled and they nodded their heads. Yes, the friends would all go and help the other animals!

TITLE: <u>Concept Cards</u>

REFERENCE: Edwards, P. (1995). <u>Concept cards: A content-area study technique</u>. Center for Educational Studies & Services, State University of New York at Plattsburgh.

DESCRIPTION: A strategy for the revision and application of important content-area knowledge through a game format.

PROCEDURE:

1.   Take one pack of playing cards and remove all color cards and the jokers. This will leave you with ten cards, from one (the ace) to ten, in each of the four suits of hearts, spades, diamonds and clubs.

2.   Select forty items of vocabulary, important terms or concepts from a unit or course you are studying and that you will need to know and understand how to use.

3.   Make four sets of randomly selected words/concepts out of the forty items and place these on a sheet of paper, an overhead transparency, or a chalk board.

4.   Name each of the four sets either hearts, spades, diamonds or clubs. (See following diagram).

5.   Each player selects a card and the one with the highest card becomes the dealer.

6.   The dealer shuffles the cards and starting from the left, deals one card, face down, to each player.

7.   The player on the dealer's left turns his/her card over and states the suit and the number of the card. (e.g. 6 of hearts).

8.   The player must now explain the word or concept that corresponds to the card that has been turned over. (e.g. the sixth item on the hearts' list).

Hearts	Spades	Diamonds	Clubs
1.	1.	1.	1.
2.	2.	2.	2.
3.	3.	3.	3.
4.	4.	4.	4.
5.	5.	5.	5.
(6).	6.	6.	6.
7.	7.	7.	7.
8.	8.	8.	8.
9.	9.	9.	9.
10.	10.	10.	10.

9. The other players act as judges and use their texts, notes and other materials to check the accuracy of the answer.

10. If the judges agree that the answer is correct, the card is turned face down again and a point is awarded. If the answer is judged incorrect, the card is left face up in front of the player and no point is awarded.

11. The next player to the left then turns over his/her card and the same procedure is repeated as many time as desired.

12. After all players and the dealer have had a turn, another round of cards is dealt and the game continues. The player with the most points at the end of the game is the winner.

TITLE: Context, Structure, Sound, Reference (CSSR)

REFERENCE: Ruddell, M.R. (1993). Teaching content reading and writing. Boston: Allyn & Bacon.

INSTRUCTIONAL LEVELS: Elementary-Middle-High School

DESCRIPTION: A strategy to learn new words by progressing through the use of context clues, structural analysis, phonic analysis and finally checking a reference source.

PROCEDURE:

(Use any of the following suggestions and combine them wherever possible to gain the meaning of unknown words).

1.   Read and attempt to find the meaning of an unknown word by using context clues in the surrounding words or sentences.

If not successful,

2.   Study the parts of the unknown word to see if prefixes, suffixes or root words help your understanding.

If not successful,

3.   Pronounce the word and try to identify it through the way it sounds.

If not successful,

4.   Use a dictionary, glossary, reference material or ask someone for assistance to find out the meaning of the unknown word.

TITLE: Details

REFERENCE: Ruddell, R.B., & Ruddell, M.R. (1995). Teaching children to read and write. Boston: Allyn & Bacon.

INSTRUCTIONAL LEVELS: Elementary-Middle-High School

DESCRIPTION: A technique to assist the reader to locate details and factual material that supports and strengthens the main idea.

PROCEDURE:

Step 1.   Locate the main idea of a paragraph in the material you are studying.

Step 2.   Look for cues that will help you find the details that support and strengthen the main idea you have selected. (See following diagram). Cues such as, "Primarily", "Secondly", "Thirdly", "Factors include", or letters and numbers such as (a), (b), (c), (1), (2), (3), will guide you in this regard.

Step 3.   Write a summary of the main idea and supporting details in indented form as shown below.

> Main Idea
>> (1) Detail
>> (2) Detail
>> (3) Detail

Step 4.   Continue reading and organizing the rest of the paragraphs in a similar manner.

DETAILS

M.I.
MAIN IDEAS

D DETAILS

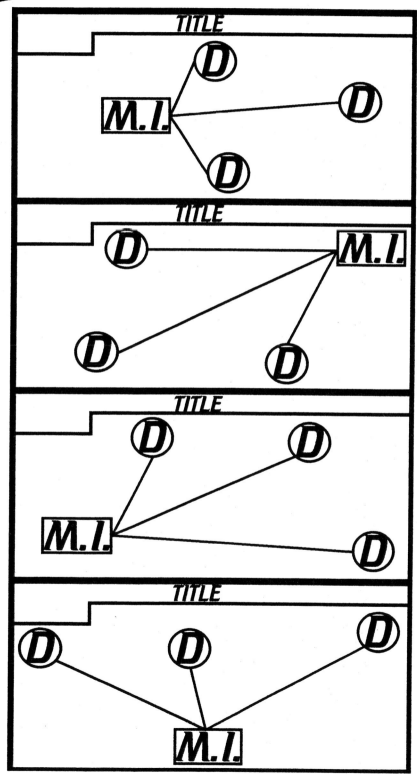

TITLE: <u>Directed Listening Thinking Activity (DLTA)</u>

REFERENCE: Stauffer, R.G. (1969). <u>Directing reading maturity as a cognitive process</u>. New York: Harper & Row.

INSTRUCTIONAL LEVELS: All levels.

DESCRIPTION: Students make predictions about material they are listening to and then check to confirm or reject their predictions.

PROCEDURE:

STEP 1:   Show the students the title and any illustrations on the cover or the beginning of the story/material to develop readiness and a purpose for listening. Ask them, "What do you think the story/material is about?"

STEP 2:   Read part of the story/material to the students and ask them to make predictions about what will happen next. "Who can think of what will happen next?"

STEP 3:   Ask the students to listen to check their predictions. "Was your prediction a good one?" "Why?" "Why not?"

STEP 4:   Ask the students to react to the story/material. "What did you think was the most exciting part?" "Why did you like it?"

STEP 5:   Develop comprehension questions and other listening skills from the story/materials.

TITLE: <u>Directed Reading Activity (DRA)</u>

REFERENCE: Betts, E.A. (1946). <u>Foundations of reading</u>
                <u>instruction.</u> New York: American Book Company.

INSTRUCTIONAL LEVELS: Primary-Elementary-Middle School.

DESCRIPTION: A structured reading approach that involves four stages: preparation, presentation, guided reading and responding. This technique is usually associated with publishers' programs (basals).

PROCEDURE:

1.   Develop the background of the story and motivate readers.

2.   Look at the cover of the book, the title and teach any difficult words that the children do not know. Ask for the meaning of words and have the children work in groups and use the words in sentences.

3.   Use directed silent and oral reading. Have the children search for answers to preset questions such as, "Do you think that the animals will escape?" or "What did the children finally do?"

4.   Develop reading skills through a variety of activities.

5.   Use enrichment activities that involve the students in the language arts.

TITLE: Directed Reading Thinking Activity (DRTA)

REFERENCE: Stauffer, R.G. (1969). Directing reading maturity as a cognitive process. New York: Harper & Row.

INSTRUCTIONAL LEVELS: All levels.

DESCRIPTION: Students make predictions about material they are going to read and then read to confirm or reject their predictions.

PROCEDURE:

STEP 1: Show the students the title and any illustrations on the cover or the beginning of the story/material to develop readiness and a purpose for reading. Ask them, "What do you think the story/material is about?"

STEP 2: Read part of the story/material to the students and ask them to make predictions about what will happen next. "Who can think of what will happen next?"

STEP 3: Ask the students to read to check their predictions. "Was your prediction a good one?" "Why?" "Why not?"

STEP 4: Ask the students to react to the story/material. "What did you think was the most exciting part?" "Why did you like it?"

STEP 5: Develop comprehension questions and other reading skills from the story/materials.

TITLE: Echo Reading

REFERENCE: Neville, M.H. (1968). Effects of oral and echoic responses in beginning reading. Journal of Educational Psychology, 59, 362-369.

INSTRUCTIONAL LEVELS: Primary-Elementary-Remedial

DESCRIPTION: Used to develop confidence and fluency in reading by modeling correct pronunciation and phrasing for the reader.

PROCEDURE:

STEP 1:   The teacher selects 200 words of text (near frustration level).

STEP 2:   The teacher reads the first line of the text with expression. Longer passages can be used if the children can manage them.

STEP 3:   The children then model the reading of the passage, pointing to the text if needed.

STEP 4:   The teacher and the children finally read the entire text together.

(Note similarity to Impress Method)

TITLE: Experience-Text-Relationship (ETR)

REFERENCE: Au, K.H. (1979). Using the experience-text-relationship method with minority children. The Reading Teacher, 32(6), 677-679.

INSTRUCTIONAL LEVELS: Originally developed for minority children but also useful for Elementary-Middle school.

DESCRIPTION: The use of a story theme that relates to the children's backgrounds to stimulate the children's interest in reading and help develop their comprehension.

PROCEDURE:

E - Experience Stage

The children discuss their experiences or background knowledge that relate to the theme of a story they are about to read that has been preselected by the teacher.

T - Text

The children silently read short passages of the story and the teacher leads a discussion by asking questions about the content. Any misunderstandings that the children have about the story are corrected by the teacher during this stage. The teacher may use a variety of questions, prompts and visual aids to help the children with their understanding of the story.

R - Relationship

The teacher guides the children into drawing relationships between the theme of the story and their own background experiences.

TITLE: <u>Give Me Space!</u>

REFERENCE: Guenther, J., & West, A. (1989). <u>It's NIE for K-3.</u>
                            Overland Park, Kansas: News Relief, Inc.

INSTRUCTIONAL LEVELS: Primary-Elementary-Middle

DESCRIPTION: Provides practice in the use of contractions (shortened
            words) and in determining their full meaning through an
            examination and discussion of comic strips and cartoons.

PROCEDURE:

1.   Select a comic strip or a cartoon that contains several
      contractions from a newspaper, magazine or book.

2.   Cut out the item (if permitted) and paste it in the space below.

3.   Circle, underline or highlight the contractions.

4.   Think about what the contractions are saying.

5.   Discuss what the contractions mean with other students, teachers,
      or adults.

6.   Write the two words that you think the contractions mean at the
      bottom of the page. (See following illustration).

7.   Check your answers in a dictionary and correct any mistakes.

GIVE ME SPACE!

Contractions:

1. shouldn't
2. wouldn't
3. you'll

Full meaning (two words):

1. should not
2. would not
3. you will

TITLE: <u>Guided Imagery</u>

REFERENCE: Walker, B.J. (1985). Right-brained strategies for
                          teaching comprehension. <u>Academic Therapy</u>, <u>21</u>, 133-141.

INSTRUCTIONAL LEVELS: Primary-Elementary-Middle

DESCRIPTION: Helps develop comprehension and stimulate background experiences through the use of sensory images in a guided storyline.

PROCEDURE:

1.   Teacher designs a guided imagery journey where the students are asked to follow the teacher's directions and imagine what is happening. (e.g. the students are told to imagine that they are walking through a field, a forest, or a town.)

2.   Teacher intersperses story with calming events such as telling the students to relax or listen for sounds or imagine smells.

3.   Students listen with their eyes closed.

4.   Students use imagination to resolve problems that may occur in the story (e.g. How to help someone they meet in the story).

5.   Students discuss their journey (story) in small groups.

6.   Students' stories are written and revised.

7.   Stories are read repeatedly to create a predictive set.

8.   Reading exercises are created using flash cards, cloze exercises and anthologies.

TITLE: Herringbone Technique

REFERENCE: Tierney, R.J., Readence, J.E., & Dishner, E.K. (1985).
                  Reading strategies and practices: A compendium (2nd ed.).
                  Boston: Allyn and Bacon.

INSTRUCTIONAL LEVELS: Elementary-Middle-High School

DESCRIPTION: A study technique involving reading, note-taking and comprehension of the main idea and supporting details.

PROCEDURE:

STEP 1:   Select reading material at the students' level.

STEP 2:   Construct a herringbone outline with the 5W's + H (Who?

               When? Where? Why? What? How?) and the main idea.

               (See following diagram).

STEP 3:   Students read, brainstorm and write important

               information about the story in their notebook.

STEP 4:   After discussion, the students write answers on

               the herringbone outline.

STEP 5:   Students discuss answers (5W+1H+main idea).

STEP 6:   The herringbone outline is used for the revision of the

               story.

The Herringbone Technique

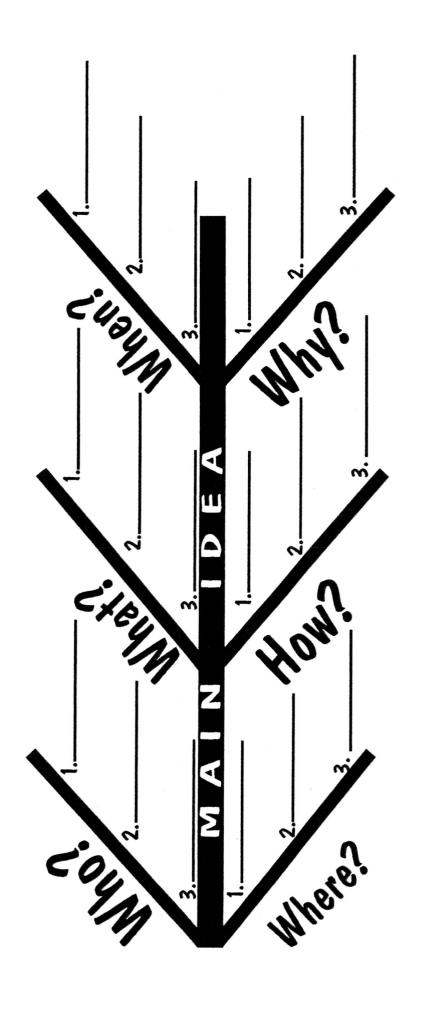

THE HERRINGBONE TECHNIQUE

Dean

WHO?

MAIN IDEA TO DELIVER THE MEDICINE TO NOME FROM Fairbanks, Alaska as fast as the team could go.

WHEN?
- Winter
- 1925

WHAT?
- Two children
- came down
- with diphtheria

WHY?
- To get
- medicine for
- the sick children.

HOW?
- A dog sled
- relay. Each team
- waited at a
- different stop.

WHERE?
- Nome,
- Alaska

WHO?
- Balto
- Gunnar

Source: The Bravest Dog Ever, by Natalie Stadiford.

TITLE: <u>Impress Method (Also known as</u>
                  <u>Neurological Impress Method: NIM)</u>

REFERENCE: Heckleman, R.G. (1966). Using the neurological impress
                  remedial technique. <u>Academic Therapy Quarterly, 1</u>, 235-239.

INSTRUCTIONAL LEVELS: Beginning readers

DESCRIPTION: Method of teaching reading, based on left and right brain
                research, where the teacher and the student read aloud in
                unison for about 15 minutes.

PROCEDURE:
1. Teacher selects reading material usually at a challenging level.
2. Teacher sits slightly behind the student on the right side.
3. Teacher and student hold the book together.
4. Teacher reads into the student's right ear.
5. Teacher uses index finger as a guide to the reading.
6. Teacher reads slightly louder and just ahead of the student.
7. Teacher explains difficult words when needed.
8. The finger movement-voice-words must all be synchronized.
9. Student takes the lead in reading when ready.
10. More difficult reading material can be used when required.

(Note similarity to Echo Reading)

TITLE: __InQuest__ (Investigative Questioning Procedure).

REFERENCE: Shoop, M. (1986). InQuest: A listening and reading comprehension strategy. __The Reading Teacher, 39__, 670-674.

INSTRUCTIONAL LEVELS: Primary-Elementary

DESCRIPTION: A strategy for combining student questioning based on the way journalists interview people, and spontaneous drama techniques. Excellent for integrating the language arts and for simulation activities.

PROCEDURE:

Step 1.   Select an interesting story and read the story up to an exciting part -- then stop.

Step 2.   Select one of the characters in the story and think of questions that you would like to ask about what has happened or what is likely to happen. Avoid questions that can be answered by a simple YES or NO. If this does happen, ask WHY?

Step 3.   Role play a news conference where someone who has read the story, (maybe an adult or the teacher to start with), takes the part of the selected character.

Step 4.   Other children take the parts of the investigative reporters and ask the character questions about the story.

Step 5.   Read further into the story and repeat the process using the same character and reporters or change to a different character and reporters.

Step 6.   Evaluate which questions were the best in explaining the story and in making the characters seem alive.

TITLE: <u>Jiffy Technique</u> (Also known as <u>Flap Books</u>).

REFERENCE: Evans, J., & Moore, J.E. (1985). <u>How to make books with children</u>. Monterey, CA: Evan-Moor.

INSTRUCTIONAL LEVELS: Primary-Elementary

DESCRIPTION: A motivational, group technique to interest children in vocabulary, setting questions, writing and comprehension.

PROCEDURE:

1.   Form groups and each group selects a well known character from a story or a symbolic figure from a season or holiday (e.g. Big Bird from *Sesame Street* , a witch representing Halloween, or an animal).

2.   Develop words or questions that relate to the character/figure.

3.   Make a paper cut-out figure of the character/figure. (See following illustration).

4.   Make a flap on the figure that hides a space for writing. (See following illustration).

5.   Write words or answers to the questions under the hidden flap on the character/figure.

6.   Challenge others to guess the words or answer the questions.

7.   Lift the flap to check their words or answers.

TITLE: <u>Journal Writing</u>

REFERENCE: Staton, J. (1980). Writing and counseling: Using a

dialogue journal. <u>Language Arts</u>, <u>57</u>, 514-518.

INSTRUCTIONAL LEVELS: Elementary-Middle-High School

DESCRIPTION: A strategy where students write their thoughts in brief,

informal notes and the teacher writes back a response, giving feedback, advice and

encouragement.

PROCEDURE:

Step 1.   Students write notes in their journal expressing their ideas, opinions,

reflections, concerns about issues and questions for the teacher.

Authentic writing that relates to their everyday lives and learning is of prime

importance. Correct spelling and syntax are not checked unless the teacher makes

note of important, specific errors that should be followed up at a later time.

Step 2.   The teacher reads the journal as soon as possible and writes

comments to the student giving feedback and encouragement, and answering

specific questions and concerns.

Step 3.   Major concerns of the student can be identified and followed up

quickly while progress can be checked continuously to monitor how the system is

working.

Step 4.   The journal (dialogue or response) acts as an external memory for the

student and the teacher that can be checked at any time.

Step 5.   Computer technology using e-mail can be used in a similar manner both

for in-class and off-campus operations.

TITLE: KWL Teaching Model

REFERENCE: Ogle, D. (1986). The KWL: A teaching model that develops active reading of expository text. The Reading Teacher, 39, 564-576.

INSTRUCTIONAL LEVELS: Elementary-Middle

DESCRIPTION: A metacognitive strategy that establishes a purpose for reading expository material and for developing comprehension.

PROCEDURE:

The symbols KWL represent the following:

K   *What do you know?*

Brainstorm all available information on the topic.

Use prior knowledge and background

Consider the source and substance of the material

Organize categories of information

W   *What do you want to learn?*

Identify areas of concern or aspects of the topic that are unclear or not known.

Develop a purpose for reading

Stress interests, needs, motivation

L   *What did you learn?*

Record information during or after reading

Teacher helps students evaluate

Use other resources if necessary

Name:_____   Date:_____

K. W. L.

What I know:	What I want to know:	What I learned:

TITLE: <u>Language Experience Approach (LEA)</u>

REFERENCE: Lee, D., & Van Allen, R. (1963). <u>Learning to read</u>
                <u>through experience</u>. New York: Meredith Publishing.

INSTRUCTIONAL LEVELS: Primary-Elementary-Middle

DESCRIPTION: The use of students' oral language in relating their experiences
to generate learning activities in literacy.

PROCEDURE:

STEP 1:   Discuss a shared, group experience such as a field trip, a

                guest speaker or a video movie.

STEP 2:   Write what the students say on a chart or large paper. (An

                alternative method is to let the children write their own

                work and make any corrections later).

STEP 3:   Make copies of the written work, either as a group story

                or as a series of individual stories.
STEP 4:   Practice reading the written work.

STEP 5:   Develop literacy skills from the story.

TITLE: <u>Main Idea</u>

REFERENCE: Ruddell, R.B., & Ruddell, M.R. (1995). <u>Teaching children to read and write</u>. Boston: Allyn & Bacon.

INSTRUCTIONAL LEVELS: Elementary-Middle-High School

DESCRIPTION: A technique to assist the reader to locate the central thought or main idea in various locations in print materials.

PROCEDURE:

Step 1. Read the material you are studying and look for the key sentence or statement that best explains the main thought of the material. The key sentence or statement may be at the beginning of the material, somewhere in the middle of the material, or toward the end of the material. (See following diagram).

Step 2. Read the rest of the paragraph and see if the main thought is repeated in any way in the material.

Step 3. Read the other sentences and see if they add details or facts to support the main idea you have selected.

Step 4. Take the sentence or statement out of the paragraph and see if it still makes sense.

MAIN IDEA

Location 1: At The Beginning - The main idea occurs at the beginning of the paragraph in most cases of good writing.

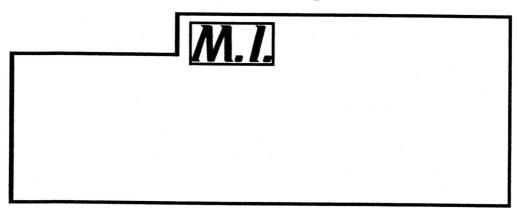

Location 2: In The Middle - Another type of paragraph has the main idea placed somewhere in the middle of the paragraph.

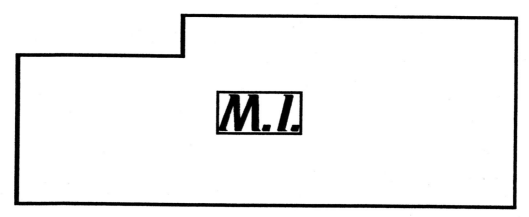

Location 3: At The End - In some cases, the "inverted form" is used and the main idea occurs at the end of the paragraph.

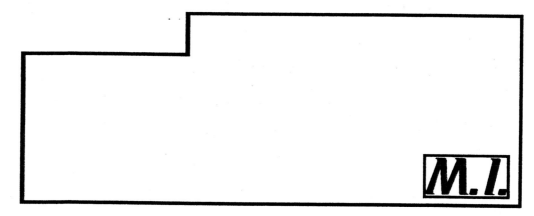

TITLE: Maze Technique

REFERENCE: Guthrie, J.T., Seifert, M., Burnham, N.A., & Caplan, R.I. (1974). The maze technique to assess, monitor reading comprehension. The Reading Teacher, 28(2), 161-168.

INSTRUCTIONAL LEVELS: Elementary-Middle

DESCRIPTION: Used to measure and monitor reading comprehension.

PROCEDURE:

1. Before giving a maze test, inform students that they will be taking a test that will measure their comprehension. Show them how the maze works on the board with sample sentences.

2. Select a reading passage of approximately 120 words from material that has not been presented in class.

3. Leave the first sentence intact. Starting with the second sentence, select at random one of the first five words and delete it. (For an easier version, delete every tenth word). Type the sentence and place two distracters (one that is the same part of speech and one that is a different part of speech) and the correct word in the blank space. Vary the positions of these words.

Examples: The girl ran very *bright/fast/in*. I saw a big *house/on/food*.

4. Delete every fifth word thereafter, until there is a total of 20 deletions. (Use 10 deletions when deleting every tenth word). Leave one more sentence intact.

5. Students are not to use their textbooks in completing the maze exercise.

6. Count as correct every <u>exact word</u> selected.

7. Use the following reading evaluation scale: Independent = 85% correct; Instructional = 60%-70% correct; Frustrated = below 50% correct.

TITLE: PANORAMA

REFERENCE: Edwards, P. (1973). PANORAMA: a study skills

technique. Journal of Reading, 17(2), 132-135.

INSTRUCTIONAL LEVELS: Middle-High School

DESCRIPTION: A three stage study technique for the content areas.

PROCEDURE:

1. Preparatory Stage

P: **Purpose for reading.** Emphasizes the need for concentration. The student must answer the questions: "Why am I studying this particular material?" Is it background material for a course? References for a term paper? Notes for a seminar or a quiz? Preparation for an exam?

A: **Adapt reading rate** to the difficulty of the material. Determine how fast to read the selection. Be prepared to be flexible in reading rate even within the selection. Don't read difficult study-type material too quickly. However, do be prepared to skim and scan certain sections.

N: **Need to make questions.** Convert titles, subheadings, statements, etc. into questions. Then read "aggressively" to find the answers. Don't be a "passive" reader. Work hard at your reading.

2. Intermediate Stage

O: **Overview.** Look for the organization of the material. Make a quick check of the following:

- author(s) and their qualifications   - year of publications

- table of contents (chapters)   - use of subheadings

- pictorial aids, graphs, etc.   - chapter summaries and tests

- evaluation section   - glossary, index

R: Read and relate. Preview, skim, scan, or read intensively as the material requires. Locate the thesis, main ideas, and supporting facts. Relate your experience and background to the material to gain meaning and understanding. Read to answer the questions you have set.

A: Annotate. Use the following system for personal books and journals, hand-outs, etc.

- Underline main ideas and supporting facts. Use a color code: e.g. red = main idea; blue = dates, numbers; yellow = facts.

-Devise a marking system (circle, box, asterisk, check, etc.) to indicate important information. Where you are not permitted to mark the reading material, use an outline system of note-taking in your workbook.

3. Concluding Stage

M: Memorize.   Organize concepts and facts into systems that will allow recall when the information is needed. (Write on small cards.)

- Make outlines and summaries that are meaningful and quickly memorized

- Develop new ways of arranging notes

- Use acronyms to memorize key points

- Use mnemonics and association methods to recall vital information

A: Assess. Finally, assess your work. Test yourself. Have you accomplished the goals that you established in the first stage of the studying technique (Purpose)? Do you have the most important information available as a result of your reading and studying? Can you recall the main ideas and most of the factual material? Most importantly - do you understand the material you have studied?

PANORAMA

P	PURPOSE FOR READING	
A	ADAPT READING RATE	I
N	NEED TO POSE QUESTIONS	PREPARATORY STAGE
O	OVERVIEW	
R	READ AND RELATE	II INTERMEDIATE STAGE
A	ANNOTATE	
M	MEMORIZE	III
A	ASSESS	CONCLUDING STAGE

TITLE: Phonogram (Rime) Method

REFERENCE: Wylie, R.E., & Durrell, D.D. (1970). Teaching

vowels through phonograms. Elementary English, 47, 787-791.

INSTRUCTIONAL LEVELS: Primary-Elementary-Remedial

DESCRIPTION: Building "word families" by adding affixes to phonograms

(rimes).

PROCEDURE:

1.   Ask children for words that contain an identical phonogram (rime):

(e.g. *an*) can, fan, man, plan.

2.   List the words and separate the initial consonant or blend from the

phonogram (rime):

                 c/**an**
                 f/**an**
                 m/**an**
                 pl/**an**

3.   Say the words and point out the phonogram (rime) in each of the

words.

4.   Highlight or underline the phonogram (rime) in a color.

5.   Say and write the words in context.

6.   Use the words in activities.

TITLE: Pictorial Outlines

REFERENCE: Edwards, P. (1996). Seven keys to successful
                 study (2nd ed.). Melbourne: Australian Council for
                 Educational Research.

INSTRUCTIONAL LEVELS: Elementary-Middle-High School

DESCRIPTION: A method of reading and note-taking where the notes are organized
in the outline of a meaningful picture or symbol that is closely related to the topic bein
studied and are therefore more easily memorized and recalled.

PROCEDURE:

1.   Make a line drawing that represents a symbol or a main object of the topic or
subject you are studying. For example, if you are reading about the values of trees you
may make a simple outline in the shape of a tree, using the large branches for the main
ideas and the smaller branches for the supporting details. (See following diagram).

2.   Place your important notes on the relevant parts of the tree outline.

3.   Study the shape of the tree and the notes you have written.

4.   Look away from your work and picture the notes you have written.

5.   Think of the notes you have written and why you placed them there.

6.   Draw the tree and write in the notes again.

7.   Check your work to see how accurate you were.

8.   Keep practicing until you can remember all of the material you need to
        know.

Pictorial Outlines

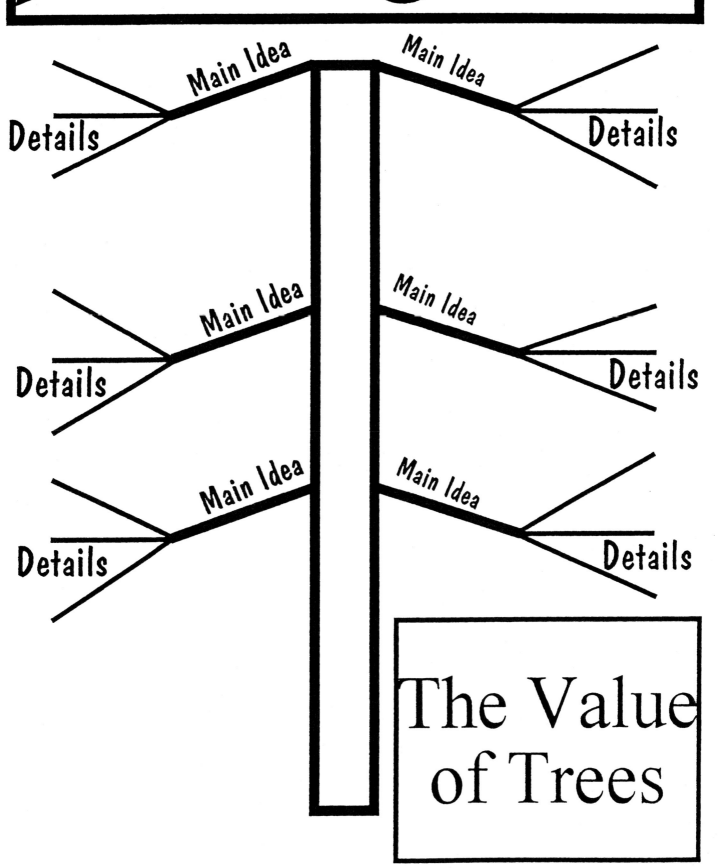

Main Idea

Main Idea

Details

Details

Main Idea

Main Idea

Details

Details

Main Idea

Main Idea

Details

Details

The Value of Trees

TITLE: **Question/Answer Relationship (QAR)**

REFERENCE: Raphael, T.E. (1982). **Teaching children question-answering strategies.** The Reading Teacher, 36(2), 186-191.

INSTRUCTIONAL LEVELS: Elementary-Middle

DESCRIPTION: Three questioning strategies to improve comprehension that involve the type of question, the textual context, and the prior knowledge of the reader.

PROCEDURE:

The three QAR strategies:

1. Right There

The reader looks for the answer to a literal, factual question by finding the sentence where words have been used to create the question and then using the other words in the sentence to provide the answer.

e.g. Dean went to the library today. Question: "Where did Dean go today?"

Answer: "To the library."

2. Think and Search

The reader needs to look at more material in a passage to find the answers to these types of questions. This may involve skimming and integrating information from a number of sentences.

3. On My Own

In this situation the reader uses prior knowledge and background experience to find answers to inferential type questions.

TITLE: <u>Readers' Theater</u>

REFERENCE: Larson, M.L. (1976). Readers' Theater: New

vitality for oral reading. <u>The Reading Teacher</u>,<u>29</u>, 359-360.

INSTRUCTIONAL LEVELS: Elementary-Middle

DESCRIPTION: An oral reading presentation of literature by children to

an audience without the use of elaborate costumes,

backdrops or props.

PROCEDURE:

1.   The teacher selects an appropriate narrative text.

2.   The teacher outlines characters, setting, events and purpose.

3.   Children select roles (characters, narrator) and parts to read.

4.   Children are given time to preview and practice the script silently.

5.   When they are ready, the children stand and read the script orally

and expressively to the audience..

6.   No props or costumes are used (optional).

7.   Listeners rely on the quality of the reading, their listening skills,

and their imagination to interpret the story.

8.   Later, the children select or write their own script.

TITLE: Reading Logs

REFERENCE: Templeton, S. (1991). Teaching the integrated

language arts. Boston: Houghton Mifflin.

INSTRUCTIONAL LEVELS: Elementary-Middle-High School

DESCRIPTION: Students write their thoughts and predictions about a story that they are reading. This technique helps develop comprehension and also allows the students to monitor their own progress.

PROCEDURE:

1.   Teacher selects appropriate stories for prediction purposes.

2.   Teacher selects and marks key points in the story.

3.   Teacher prepares log sheets. (See following diagram).

4.   After the student reads, the logs are used for discussion.

5.   Students discuss their interpretation of the story and how their

learning developed during the reading.

6.   Students discuss the influence of their background and their

personal experiences on their comprehension.

Reading Logs

Name_____   Date_____

Today, I would like to read:_____

Here is how I liked the story:_____

Let me tell you about it:_____

_____

_____

_____

_____

Here is a picture of someone or something in the story.

Next, I would like to read:_____

_____

TITLE: Rebus Writing

REFERENCE: Danielson, K.E., & LaBonty, J. (1994). <u>Integrating</u>
<u>reading and writing through children's literature.</u>
Boston: Allyn & Bacon.

INSTRUCTIONAL LEVELS: Primary-Elementary-Remedial

DESCRIPTION: Words and pictures of difficult or non-sight words are
interspersed in children's writing.

PROCEDURE:

1.   A story or experience is described orally.

2.   The story is written on large paper.

Example: *One day a **girl** went for a **walk** in the zoo. She saw a **lion**,*

*a **monkey**, a **bird** and a **rabbit**. She really wanted to see a large*

***elephant** or a **horse**, but they were not there.*

3.   Non-sight words or difficult words are replaced with pictures.

The pictures may be cut out from magazines or drawn by the

children. (See example on following page).

4.   Students read the story (words and pictures).

5.   The pictures are gradually replaced with their correct words.

6.   Students practice sight words, fluency, and comprehension.

REBUS WRITING

One day, a [girl] went for a [walk] in the zoo. She saw a [cat], a [monkey], a [bird], and a [rabbit]. She really wanted to see a large [elephant] or a [horse], but they were not there.

TITLE: Reciprocal Questioning (ReQuest) Procedure

REFERENCE: Manzo, A.V. (1969). The ReQuest procedure. Journal of Reading, 13, 123-126.

INSTRUCTIONAL LEVELS: Elementary-Middle

DESCRIPTION: A technique to develop students' questioning and comprehension abilities through teacher modeling.

PROCEDURE:

1.   Teacher selects an appropriate text for prediction purposes.

2.   Teacher notes points in text for asking questions.

3.   Teacher explains ReQuest procedure of asking questions.

4.   Student and teacher silently read the first sentence.

5.   Student asks teacher a question and teacher explains the answer.

6.   Teacher repeats the process.

7.   Teacher provides feedback to the student throughout the procedure.

8.   After several paragraphs the student reads the rest of the story silently and answers questions.

9.   Discussion and activities follow.

TITLE: Repeated Readings

REFERENCE: Samuels, S.J. (1979). The method of repeated

readings. Reading Teacher, 32(4), 403-408.

INSTRUCTIONAL LEVELS: General

DESCRIPTION: Students repeatedly read a short, meaningful passage of

interesting material until a satisfactory level of fluency is achieved.

PROCEDURE:

1.   Select a passage of 50-200 words.

2.   The student practices reading the selection.

3.   The student is then timed and the rate of reading and word

recognition errors are graphed on a chart. (See following diagram).

4.   The student then re-reads the material with the teacher or another

student, or practices alone.

5.   The process is repeated.

6.   When a satisfactory reading rate is achieved, (85 wpm is the

suggested rate), another selection is provided.

7.   Comprehension questions can be used if required, but the main aim

is to improve fluency and word recognition.

Repeated Readings

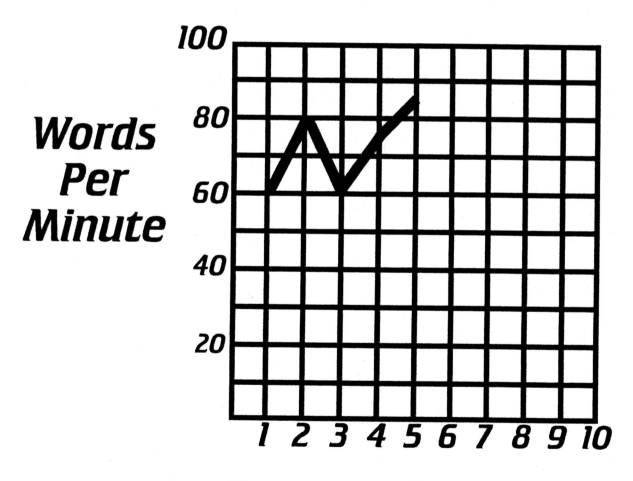

TITLE: <u>Scaffolding</u>

REFERENCE: Ogle, D., Palincsar, A., Jones, B.F., Carr, E., &
                 Ransom, K. (1986). <u>Teaching reading as thinking</u>.
                 Alexandria, VA: Association for Symposium and
                 Curriculum Development.

INSTRUCTIONAL LEVELS: Beginning reading

DESCRIPTION: The teacher supplies considerable support in initial reading
instruction and gradually reduces the support as the learner becomes more
proficient in reading.

PROCEDURE:

1. **Support**   Scaffolding is provided by supporting the student's
              attempts to read. The support can be verbal, written,
         through the use of graphics, or by any other means that
         assist the reader.

2. **Modeling** The correct procedures and reading strategies are
         modeled for the reader as required.

3. **Adjusting**   The amount and level of support given is adjusted
              depending on the needs of the reader, the nature of the
         learning tasks and the nature of the instructional
         material being used.

4. **Monitoring**   The progress of the reader is continuously monitored as
              the instruction takes place.

TITLE: <u>Schema Theory</u>

REFERENCE: Hacker, C.J. (1980). From schema theory to

classroom practice. <u>Language Arts, 57</u>, 866-871.

INSTRUCTIONAL LEVELS: Elementary-Middle-High School

DESCRIPTION: Uses the knowledge networks and background experiences of an individual's mental framework to relate to new learning situations and to develop literacy skills.

PROCEDURE:

STAGE 1. SELECTION:

All available knowledge relating to a topic, concept, or term is selected. e.g. When given the term *flower,* an individual may associate the following information: plant, rose, carnation, stem, petals, beauty, color, decorations, wreaths, smell.

STAGE 2. DEVELOPMENT:

The knowledge can then be organized into specific categories such as names of flowers, parts of flowers, appearance and uses of flowers, and used in the main idea and the details/vocabulary sections of the following diagram.

STAGE 3. REVISION:

The knowledge can finally be revised and further developed as additional information is obtained and then used in a variety of learning situations to improve literacy skills.

Reading & Language Schema

Main Idea

Details / Vocabulary:

Main Idea

Details / Vocabulary:

Topic

Main Idea

Main Idea

Details / Vocabulary:

Main Idea

Details / Vocabulary:

Details / Vocabulary:

TITLE: Scrambled Stories

REFERENCE: Whaley, J.F. (1981). Story grammars and reading
                 instruction. The Reading Teacher, 34(7), 762-771.
INSTRUCTIONAL LEVELS: Primary-Elementary-Middle
DESCRIPTION: Teaching sequence and comprehension by having children
correctly re-assemble a story from a number of jumbled story parts.

1.   Select an appropriate story and separate it into a number of parts.

2.   Place the story parts on pieces of cardboard or stiff paper.

3.   Make a correct sequence of events for checking and then jumble the

story parts. Erase any page numbers that are visible. (See illustration).

4.   Select a reader and a number of children for each of the story parts.

5.   Give each child (except the story reader) a story part.

6.   The children meet as a group and examine the various story parts

      in order to place them in the correct order to make sense of the story.
7.   When they have decided on the correct sequence of story parts, the

      children form a line in the front of the room and display their story parts.

8.   The story reader then reads the story in the sequence that the

      children have agreed on.

9.   When errors in the sequence are found, the children re-arrange their

      order and repeat the process until the correct sequence is found.

Scrambled Story

TITLE: <u>Semantic Feature Analysis</u> (or <u>Feature Analysis</u>)

REFERENCES: Katz, J.J. (1972). <u>Semantic theory.</u> New York:
Harper & Row.

Johnson, T.D., & Pearson, P.D. (1978). <u>Teaching</u>
<u>reading vocabulary</u>. New York: Holt, Rinehart &
Winston.

INSTRUCTIONAL LEVELS: Elementary-Middle-High School

DESCRIPTION: Develops vocabulary and categorizing ability through the
analysis of similarities and differences in words and concepts.

PROCEDURE:

1.   Select a category that is familiar to the children: e.g. sport.

2.   Children list names, words and concepts that belong to the category: e.g.
names of various sports such as boxing, football, diving, basketball, golf.

3.   Teacher now selects features that are common or distinct to the
sports: e.g. team sport, individual sport, contact sport, water sport, ball
sport.

4.   Teacher now develops a matrix containing the sports and the features and
guides the children in identifying which sport has any of the features. (See
following diagram).

5.   Children place a + or a - to indicate which feature belongs to each sport.

6.   Children may add other sports and/or features to the matrix as they wish.

7.   Children explore the matrix and analyze the various similarities and
differences among the sports selected for discussion..

Semantic Feature Analysis

Sport	Team Sport	Individual Sport	Contact Sport	Ball Sport	Water Sport
Football	+	-	+	+	-
Diving	-	+	-	-	+
Basketball	+	-	-	+	-
Golf	-	+	-	+	-
Boxing	-	+	+	-	-

TITLE: <u>Similes</u>

REFERENCE: Readence, J.E., Baldwin, R.S., & Rickelman, R.J. (1983). Instructional insights into metaphors and similes. <u>Journal of Reading, 27</u>, 109-112.

INSTRUCTIONAL LEVELS: Elementary-Middle

DESCRIPTION: Similes are used to develop children's descriptive use of language by comparing and contrasting the characteristics of known objects and concepts.

(Metaphors can be used in a similar manner).

PROCEDURE:

1.   The teacher selects a key word or concept, that can be used in a simile, from any content-area material.

Example: *A tornado*

2.   The teacher creates a simile to describe the word or concept.

Example: *A tornado is like a giant, spinning top.*

3.   The teacher explains how the simile is similar and/or different.

Example: *A tornado may have the shape or appearance of a spinning top (similar), but a tornado is not made of solid material (different).*

4.   Students create their own similes for words or concepts.

5.   Students explain how their simile is similar and/or different.

6.   Students discuss the meaning and imagery of the words or concepts.

TITLE: <u>SQ3R</u>

REFERENCE: Robinson, F. (1961). <u>Effective study</u> (Rev. ed.).

New York: Harper Row.

INSTRUCTIONAL LEVELS: Elementary-Middle-High School

DESCRIPTION: A higher-level study technique that teaches students how to extract information from content-area material through a series of carefully planned steps.

PROCEDURE:

The symbols SQ3R represent the following:

1. **S (Survey)**   Look over the headings and the subheadings in the material you are to read to see which main points are going to be developed. Also read the final summary if there is one.

2. **Q (Question)**   Turn all headings and sub-headings into questions. This action changes passive reading of the material into active reading.

3. **R (Read)** Read actively to find the answers to the questions you have posed.

4. **R (Recite)**   Attempt to answer the questions in your own words. Give examples wherever possible and make brief notes to assist your study.

5. **R (Review)**   Go over the material again and check to see if you have covered the main points and the supporting details thoroughly.

TITLE:　　　　　　Story Frames

REFERENCE:　　　Fowler, G.L. (1982). Developing comprehension skills in primary students through the use of story frames. The Reading Teacher, 36(2), 176-179.

INSTRUCTIONAL LEVELS:　Primary-Elementary (Remedial)

DESCRIPTION:　An outline framework that gives the student assistance in writing and comprehension by providing key words at various stages in a story (e.g. plot summary, setting, character analysis, character comparison, and the solution to the story's problem).

PROCEDURE:

1.　Select a suitable story or passage that involves one of the following: a story summary with one character included, a problem or conflict, a setting, a character analysis, or a character comparison.

2.　As the story is read, the children are asked if there is a problem or conflict in the story. The problem or conflict may involve the plot or the setting of the story, or the facts in a passage.

3.　Select a paragraph that deals with the problem or conflict.

4.　Delete everything in the paragraph except the words, phrases or sentences needed to maintain the purpose of the paragraph. You may need to make a notation under some of the deletions such as a character's name or a characteristic so that the reader will be able to understand the frame more easily. (e.g. I think that

_____ is _____

(character's name)　　　　　　(afraid)

because _____.

5. Use the frame with other stories or passages that deal with similar themes or issues to the one that was selected.

6. Adapt the frame to other content-area passages. [See Hoblitt, R., & Walton, S. (1989). Using story frames in content-area classes. The Social Studies, 80, 103-106].

****

Story Frame Activity (General)

****

In this story, the problem starts when _____

_____

_____

_____

_____.

After that, _____

_____

_____.

Next, _____

_____

_____.Then,

_____

_____. The

problem is finally solved when _____

_____

_____. The story ends _____

_____.

TITLE: Story Graphs

REFERENCE: Edwards, P. (1996). Seven keys to successful

study (2nd ed.). Melbourne: Australian Council for

Educational Research.

INSTRUCTIONAL LEVELS: Elementary-Middle-High School

DESCRIPTION: A simple line graph that shows the interest level (or the importance to the plot) of the main incidents or events in a story.

PROCEDURE:

1.   Draw the framework for a line graph. Construct a vertical axis and a horizontal axis.

2.   Mark equal intervals along the vertical axis to show the interest or importance of the story.

3.   Mark equal intervals along the horizontal axis to show the incidents or main points of the story. (Use a "key" box to list the main points).

4.   Draw lines from each of the interval points to construct a grid network. (If you are using graph paper this is already done for you).

5.   Plot the incidents of the story on the grid (graph).

6.   Draw a line connecting each of the incidents into a line graph. (See following diagram).

STORY GRAPH

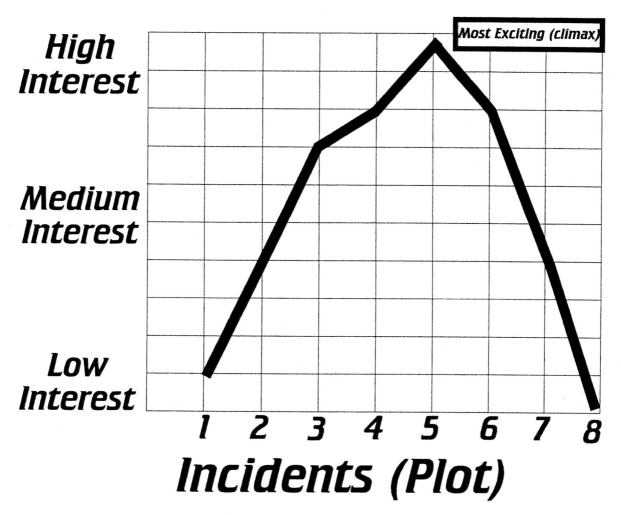

High Interest

Medium Interest

Low Interest

Most Exciting (Climax)

Incidents (Plot)

Main Points:

1. A starship leaves Earth to explore.
2. A wormhole pulls the ship off course.
3. The starship is attacked by an alien vessel.
4. The attack kills some of the crew.
5. The hero fights and destroys the alien vessel.
6. The starship is badly damaged.
7. The starship is repaired.
8. The starship returns to Earth.

TITLE: <u>Story Maps</u>

REFERENCE: Davis, Z.T. & McPherson, M.D. (1989) Story map

                  instruction: A road map for reading comprehension. <u>The</u>

                  <u>Reading Teacher,</u> <u>43</u>(3), 232-240.

INSTRUCTIONAL LEVELS: Primary-Elementary

DESCRIPTION: This technique allows children to review the events in a story

either through the use of pictures or a written outline.

PROCEDURE:

1.   Teacher selects a narrative story with a cohesive story line. This

usually involves the setting (characters, time and place); the problem or

conflict in the story; attempts and results of trying to solve the problem

 or conflict; the outcome of these efforts; and the conclusion and/or

moral of the story.

2.   Teacher prepares questions to lead students through the story map.

3.   Teacher explains organizational structure of the story.

4.   Teacher explains use of the visual story map. (See following diagram).

5.   Students read story.

6.   Teacher and students complete map together using teacher

        questions. (See the example using *Arthur's Birthday* by Marc Brown).

7.   Teacher and students compare their story maps with one another.

STORY MAP

Setting:

Main Characters	Time	Place

Problem:

Attempts To Solve Problem: **Results:**

1.   1.

2.   2.

3.   3.

Outcome:

Moral:

STORY MAP

Setting:

Main Characters: Arthur, Muffy, Francine

Time: May

Place: Arthur's home and at school.

Problem: Arthur and Muffy have a birthday party on the same day.

Attempts To Solve Problem:

1. The boys have a meeting at school.

2. The girls have a playground meeting.

3. Arthur and Francine come up with a solution to have a surprise party for Muffy.

Results:

1. The boys decide that they should go to Arthur's party.

2. The girls decide to go to Muffy's.

3. Arthur and Francine decide to send a special note to Muffy.

Outcome: All of the friends meet at Arthur's place and celebrate the two parties together.

Moral: True friends can solve problems and remain friends.

TITLE: Story Mobiles

REFERENCE: Norton, D. (1985). Language arts activities for
                children. New York, NY: Houghton Mifflin.

INSTRUCTIONAL LEVELS: Primary-Elementary

DESCRIPTION: A strategy that allows children to use written
        expression and art work to express their knowledge
        and opinion of material they have studied.

PROCEDURE:

Step 1.   Select an interesting story and prepare the necessary
                materials that include construction paper or cardboard, a hole
                punch, yarn, markers, and a coat hanger.

Step 2.   Read the story and make a story map that includes the title,
                author, main characters, setting, problem, turning point, and
                solution.

Step 3.   Cut out a different shape of construction paper or cardboard
                for the title, author, and the story elements.
                (See following diagram).

Step 4.   Use the story map and print the information on each of the
                shapes.

Step 5.   Draw a picture on the other side of the shape to match
                the print information.

Step 6.   Punch holes at the top and the bottom of each of the
                shapes.

Step 7.   Connect the shapes in order to the coat hanger.

Step 8.   Use the story mobile to retell the story.

STORY MOBILE

Title: <u>A New Coat for Anna</u>.

Author: Harriet Ziefert.

Main Characters

Anna and
Anna's mother

Setting

Germany after
World War II.

Problem

Anna needs a
new coat for winter.

Turning Point

Anna's mother comes up
wih the idea of bartering to
get a coat for Anna.

SOLUTION

Anna's mother has a tailor make
a new red coat as a Christmas
present for Anna.

TITLE: <u>Sustained Silent Reading (SSR)</u>

REFERENCE: Hunt, L.C. (1970). Effect of self-selection, interest and motivation upon independent, instructional and frustration levels. <u>The Reading Teacher, 24</u>, 146-151.

INSTRUCTIONAL LEVELS: All levels

DESCRIPTION: Designed to develop good reading habits by providing a quiet, uninterrupted reading period, modeled by <u>everyone</u> in the building, without any follow-up activities.

PROCEDURE:

STEP 1:   At a given time, <u>everyone</u> reads silently. The best times are usually after lunch or at the end of the day.

STEP 2:   <u>Everyone</u> selects their own material. (Adults can restrict certain materials if warranted).

STEP 3:   Reading time is short--usually about 15 - 20 minutes. The children are free to look at pictures or browse through selections, <u>but they must be quiet</u>.

STEP 4:   No reports or records are made by the children or the teacher.

TITLE: Synthetic Phonics

REFERENCE: Bond, G.L., & Dykstra, R. (1967). The cooperative research program in first-grade reading instruction. Reading Research Quarterly, 2(4), 5-142.

INSTRUCTIONAL LEVELS: Beginning Reading

DESCRIPTION: Speech sounds (phonemes) of selected letters and combinations of letters or word parts (graphemes) are taught first and then the various sounds are blended together to form words.

PROCEDURE:

1. Select words that contain a sound that needs to be developed; e.g. select ship, shop, shut, dash, cash to teach the sh digraph.

2. Teach the digraph first. Write sh on the board and ask the children to say it.

3. Practice saying the other sounds of the words in a similar manner.

4. Show them how to blend some of the sounds to make a word.

5. Practice saying the word.

6. Practice writing the word.

7. Place the word in context.

8. Use the word in context.

Example: Teach the digraph sh , the sounds of the vowels a, i, o, u, and the consonants c, d, p, t.

Select the digraph sh, the vowel i and the consonant p.

Say each part. Blend the parts together-- say the word sh -i -p.

Write the word: ship. Sentence work; "I saw a big ship".

Practice: Use the word ship in activities.

Extension Work: Use other words containing the digraph sh (e.g. shop, shut, dash, cash) in a similar manner.

TITLE: <u>Visual, Auditory, Kinesthetic, Tactile (VAKT)</u>
          (Also known as the <u>Multisensory Approach</u>)

REFERENCE: Fernald, G. (1943). <u>Remedial techniques in basic
              school subjects</u>. New York: McGraw Hill.

INSTRUCTIONAL LEVELS: Beginning Reading-Remedial
DESCRIPTION: A multisensory technique to teach words and letters.

PROCEDURE:
STEP 1:   Display a word (or letter) that needs to be learned on a
           card in large, dark print. (Visual)
           Make the letters out of sandpaper, or use sugar or salt
           to make the letters rough and easy to touch and feel.

STEP 2:   Trace each letter with a finger over the rough surface
           and say the sound of the letter. (Tactile and auditory)

STEP 3:   Trace the word with a finger and say the word. (Tactile
           and auditory)

STEP 4:   Write and say the word without seeing the copy.
           (Kinesthetic and auditory)

STEP 5:   Check for accuracy. (Visual)

STEP 6:   Learn the words without tracing.

TITLE: Vocabulary Self-collection Strategy (VSS)

REFERENCE: Haggard, M.R. (1982). The vocabulary self-collection strategy: An active approach to word learning. Journal of Reading, 26(4), 203-207.

INSTRUCTIONAL LEVELS: Middle-High School

DESCRIPTION: An instructional technique to develop vocabulary by adding new content-area words that a student needs to know. The students are given the opportunity to actively search for the words to be learned.

PROCEDURE:

1.   Each student reads the material and selects a word to learn:
    a)   the student tells where the word is located;
    b)   the student says what they think the word means in context;
    c)   the student gives reasons for including the word.

2.   The students attempt the meaning of the words through context.

3.   The students refine definitions of the words where needed.

4.   The students record words and definitions on cards or in their notebooks.

5.   Use words in games, activities and assessment of understanding.

TITLE: Voice-Pointing

REFERENCE: Morris, R.D. (1989). The relationship between
                word awareness and phoneme awareness in
                learning to read: A longitudinal study in
                kindergarten. Appalachian State University,
                Boone, NC.

INSTRUCTIONAL LEVELS: Primary-Remedial

DESCRIPTION: Point to a word in a line of print that has been
                memorized orally and say the word at the same time.

PROCEDURE:

1.   Children memorize a line of prose, poetry or a song.

2.   Demonstrate how to voice-point by reading aloud and pointing to each word
       in the line of print.

3.   Children then voice-point in a similar manner.

4.   Individual words can be isolated with cards or pointed to by the
       teacher and practiced by the children.

5.   Children's work can be printed in large letters on chart paper, chalk board
or   overhead transparency and voice-pointed by the children.

TITLE: <u>Wanted Poster</u>

REFERENCE: Johnson, T.D., & Louis, D.R. (1990). <u>Bringing it all together.</u> Portsmouth, NH: Heinemann.

INSTRUCTIONAL LEVELS: Elementary-Middle

DESCRIPTION: Integrates all of the language arts and creative art work through the use of humorous "Wanted" posters.

PROCEDURE:

Modeling.   Make a "wanted" poster (see following illustration) from a well known story and show it to the children. Read the words aloud and look at the pictures. Ask them what information comes from the story and what parts have been made up.

Processing. Prepare a "wanted" report form (see below) and read another story aloud to the children. Give each child a report form and have the children fill in some of the items.

Guided Practice. The children then fill in the remainder of the report form with help from the teacher and their peers.

Oral Revision. The children share their completed report forms with the other children.

Poster Session. The children work independently, in pairs or in small groups and complete their own "wanted" poster using information (writing and art work) taken from the report form.

****

WANTED REPORT FORM

****

Who/What is wanted? _____.

Why are they wanted? _____

_____.

Their appearance

Age _____ Height _____ Weight _____ Looks _____

Skin type: _____ Hair: _____ Eyes: _____

Teeth: _____ Strange Features: _____

_____.

Habits: _____

_____.

Favorite Foods: _____.

Action (What should you do if you see this character?)

_____.

Warning (Be careful of these things): _____

_____.

Reward for capturing? _____.

Things you could do with the character _____

_____

_____.

Your Name: _____   Title: _____

Signature: _____   Date: _____

****

WANTED POSTER

NAME:_____

WANTED FOR:_____

APPEARANCE:

HEIGHT:_____   AGE:_____

WEIGHT:_____   CLOTHING:_____

HAIR:_____   EYES:_____

THIS CHARACTER IS DANGEROUS BECAUSE:_____

_____

IF YOU SEE THIS CHARACTER, YOU SHOULD:_____

_____

REWARD:_____

IF YOU SEE THIS CHARACTER, CONTACT:_____

SIGNATURE:_____

BIBLIOGRAPHY

Allan, K. K., & Miller, M. S. (2000). <u>Literacy and learning: Strategies for middle and secondary school teachers</u>. Boston: Houghton Mifflin.

Allington, R., & Cunningham, P. (2002). <u>Schools that work: Where all children read and write.</u> (2nd. ed.). New York: Longman.

Alvermann, D. E. & Phelps, S. F. (2002). <u>Content reading and literacy</u>. Boston: Allyn & Bacon.

Barr, R., & Johnson, B. (1997). <u>Teaching reading in elementary classrooms.</u> (2nd ed.). New York: Longman.

Burns, P.C., Roe, B. D., & Ross, E. P. (2002). <u>Teaching reading in today's elementary schools</u>. (8th ed.). Boston: Houghton Mifflin.

Crawley, S. J., & Mountain, L. (1995). <u>Strategies for guiding content reading.</u> Boston: Allyn & Bacon.

Cunningham, P. M., Moore, S. A., Cunningham, J.W., & Moore, D.W. (2000). <u>Reading and writing in elementary classrooms: Strategies and observations.</u> (4th ed.). New York: Longman.

Eanes, R. (1997). <u>Content area literacy: Teaching for today and tomorrow.</u> Albany, NY: Delmar Publishers.

Edwards, P. (1996). <u>Seven keys to successful study</u>. (2nd ed.). Melbourne: Australian Council for Educational Research.

Gunning, T. G. (2003). <u>Building literacy in the content areas</u>. Boston: Allyn & Bacon.

Guthrie, J. T., & Wigfield, A. (Eds.). (1997). <u>Reading engagement: Motivating readers through integrated instruction.</u> Newark, DE: International Reading Association.

Harris, T. L., & Hodges, R. E. (1995). <u>The literacy dictionary: The vocabulary of reading and writing</u>. Newark, Delaware: International Reading Association.

Heilman, A. W., Blair, T. R., & Rupley, W. H. (2002). <u>Principles and practices of teaching reading.</u> (10th ed.). Upper Saddle River, NJ: Merrill/Prentice Hall.

Hennings, D. G. (2002). <u>Communication in action: Teaching the language arts</u>. (8th ed.). Boston: Houghton Mifflin.

Lauritzen, C., & Jaeger, M (1997). <u>Integrating learning through story.</u> Albany, NY: Delmar Publishers.

Leu, D. J., Jr., & Kinzer, C. K. (1999). <u>Effective reading instruction, K-8.</u> (4th ed.). Upper Saddle River, NJ: Merrill/Prentice Hall.

Manzo, A. V., & Manzo, U. C. (1994). <u>Teaching children to be literate.</u> Fort Worth, TX: Harcourt Brace Jovanovich.

May, F. B., & Rizzardi, L. (2002). <u>Reading as communication.</u> (6th ed.). Upper Saddle River, NJ: Merrill/Prentice Hall.

Moore, D. W., Moore, S. A., Cunningham, P. M., & Cunningham, J. W. (2003). <u>Developing readers and writers in the content areas K-12.</u>(4th. ed.): Boston: Allyn & Bacon.

Richardson, J. S., Morgan, R. F. (2003). <u>Reading to learn in the content areas</u>. (5th ed.). Belmont, CA: Wadsworth.

Ruddell, R. B. (2002). <u>Teaching children to read and write.</u> (3rd. ed.). Boston: Allyn & Bacon.

Ruddell, R. B., & Ruddell, M. R. (2002). <u>Teaching children to read and write.</u> (3rd ed.) Boston: Allyn & Bacon.

Searfoss, L. W., & Readence, J. E. (2001). <u>Helping children learn to read.</u> (4th ed.). Boston: Allyn & Bacon.

Templeton, S. T. (1997). <u>Teaching the integrated language arts</u>. (2nd ed.). Boston: Houghton Mifflin.

Tierney, R. J., Readence, J. E., & Dishner, E. K. (2000). <u>Reading strategies and practices.</u> (5th ed.). Boston: Allyn & Bacon.

Tomkins, G. E. (1998). <u>Language arts: Content and teaching strategies</u>. Upper Saddle River, NJ: Merrill/Prentice Hall.

Vacca, J. A., & Vacca, R. T. (2002). <u>Content area reading</u> (7th ed.). Boston: Allyn & Bacon

Vacca, J. A., Vacca, R. T., & Gove, M. K. (1995). <u>Reading and learning to read.</u> (7th ed.). New York: Harper Collins.

Valmont, W. J. (2003). <u>Technology for literacy and learning</u>. Boston: Houghton Mifflin Co.

Vukelich, C., Christie, J., & Enz, B. (2002). <u>Helping young children learn language and literacy.</u> Boston: Allyn & Bacon.

Wells, G. (1990). Creating the conditions to encourage literate thinking. <u>Educational Leadership, 47</u>(6), 13-17.

Zintz, M. V., & Maggart, Z. R. (1989). <u>The reading process: The teacher and the learner</u>. (5th ed.). Dubuque, Iowa: William C. Brown.

Internet Web Sites

The third edition of *Literacy Techniques* continues to develop the section dealing with computer web sites. However, the field of computer technology is changing so rapidly that many references that we use today may not be available tomorrow. A number of search tools such as *ask.com, altavista.com, google.com, yahoo.com, mckinley.com, einet.com, looksmart.com, netscape.com, infoseek.com, excite.com, lycao.com, hotbot.com, and webcrawler.com,* enable us to link up with a myriad of educational web sites and allow us to keep abreast of the constantly changing selections.

The following web sites (arranged alphabetically) are ones that have proved to be very useful to literacy educators in the past. They are offered in the hope that they will still be available for use in the future.

Disclaimer

Please remember that the author has no control over the content of web sites and links that are presented in this book. Every care has been taken to ensure the suitability of the material in this book at the time of printing.

www.abcteach.com   Suitable for teachers, parents, and children. The web site includes a variety of free, printable activities, help with research and report writing, ideas for projects, and diorama themes.

www.acs.ucalgary.ca/~dkbrown   *The Children's Literature Web Guide* originates at the University of Calgary in Canada and is highly rated by teachers. The site features a vast array of links dealing with Internet resources for children, teachers, parents, and young adults.

www.ajkids.com   One of the most widely used and respected web sites. Offers educational, teaching tools, help with homework, plus numerous "safe" sites for children. Includes sections on study tools and study advice.

www.atozteacherstuff.com   Provides free online lesson plans and ideas, plus activities for Pre K – 12.

www.bsu.edu/CTT/webquest.html   Enables teachers to generate WebQuest electronic lessons which can be shared by others.

www.cal.org   Center for Applied Linguistics: suitable for research into language acquisition, bilingualism, ESL, databases, articles and directories.

www.carolhurst.com   Deals mainly with children's literature. The site includes: *reviews of great books for kids.., ways to use them in the classroom.., and collections of books and activities about particular subjects, curriculum areas, themes, and professional topics.*

www.childfun.com   Includes are over 30 web sites dealing with special days, seasons, crafts, parenting advice, product and book reviews, and family articles.

www.clexchange.org   The Creative Learning Exchange *advocates systems education through learner-centered learning,* and distributes ideas and materials from primary and secondary teachers to other educators.

www.col-ed.org/cur/lang.html   Provides over 600 lesson plans and web activities prepared by teachers and suitable for language arts, math, science, social studies, and miscellaneous topics.

www.connectingstudents.com   Offers a variety of themes, literacy selections, worksheets, and lesson plans. Also included are interactive web sites and teacher resources. Highly rated by teachers.

www.crayola.com   Presents ideas and activities for teachers and parents to help children with their learning.

www.creativeclassroom.org   Designed for teachers of grades K-8, this site offers teaching strategies, time-saving ideas, and useful information from issues of *Creative Classroom*, a magazine for elementary school teachers.

www.creativeteachingsite.com   A non-profit site designed to promote creative teaching through articles, ideas and information for educators.

www.edu4kids.com   This site provides games and drills to help children improve their skills in language, math, social studies, and science.

www.eduplace.com   Gives children practice in the use of nouns and verbs in writing. Children in grades 3 and above select a title and complete a humorous story.

www.EnchantedLearning.com   Contains a wealth of information on a wide variety of topics including dinosaurs, holidays, map reading, the use of the Internet, and various research topics.

www.funbrain.com   Concentrates on games, activities, and quizzes for K-8 students and teachers. There is also a section for parents to enable them to participate in their children's education through a variety of games and activities.

www.gigglepoetry.com   A wide variety of poems and activities for children, including how to write poems , poetry contests, and teaching suggestions for teachers.

www.hvmaterialsexchange.com   A collection of lesson plans for art, language arts, math/science/technology, social studies, and economics.

www.ilovethatteachingidea.com   Provides elementary school teachers *with creative, practical, effective ideas and techniques* to assist children with learning tasks.

www.isomedia.com/homes/jmele/homepage.html   Aims to present a qualitative selection of multicultural books for K-12 educators.

www.kididdles.com   A site that contains access to a wide variety of songs, lyrics, and music for teaching purposes.

www.kidsdomain.com   *Provides an extensive selection of shareware, freeware, and demonstrations in PC and Macintosh formats for most content areas and all age groups. One of the most popular web sites for teachers.*

www.kidspsych.org   A series of puzzles and games designed for parents to play with their children (aged 1-9 years). The activities are designed to help the children develop cognitive thinking skills and deductive reasoning while they are having fun.

www.knownet.net   Contains over 100 lesson plans and ideas for spelling, writing, English, reading, and vocabulary for grades 5-6.

www.lala.essortment.com   Offers a variety of activities and games in literacy, numeracy, art, science, and other subject areas.

www.learningpage.com   Provides printable lesson plans, worksheets, and activities for Preschool K & grades 1-3.

| www.LessonPlanz.com | Free lesson plans and ideas for all grades and subjects. |

www.LessonPlanz.com   Free lesson plans and ideas for all grades and subjects.

www.marcopolo.worldcom.com   Developed by the Federal Government and private business, this program provides, *no-cost, standards-based Internet content including: Economics, Geography, Humanities, Mathematics, Science, and the Arts, for the K-12 teacher and classroom.*

www.pbskids.com   Contains *Fun & Games, Did You Know? Write On,* and 24 other PBS kids' sites. Deals with popular literature including such favorites as *Barney, Clifford,* and *Mr Rogers.*

www.perpetualpreschool.com   Presents a number of holiday themes, seasonal themes, theme resources, teacher resources, and also offers free games, greeting cards, comics, and planning tools.

www.pinkmonkey.com   States that it is: *the premier Internet study site and the world's largest provider of free literature notes on over 340 titles.* Caters to grades 6-12 and also to college students.

www.poetryzone.ndirect.co.uk/links2.htm   A UK site that specializes in poetry and offers students and teachers a variety of lesson plans, worksheets, teaching ideas, and a number of useful links to other web sites.

www.proteacher.com   Provides lesson plans, teaching resources, and web-links, plus *tens of thousands of teaching ideas on a new Teaching Ideas Archive.*

www.quia.com   Claims to be the Web's largest learning resource with over 1,000,000 activities. Includes information about educators, publishers, colleges/universities/K-12 schools, students & independent learners, and corporations.

www.readinga-z.com — For a fee, this site provides a balanced approach to literacy by providing a rich selection of resources that will help children become fluent readers. The site includes a free preview of 28 books, with accompanying lesson plans and worksheets that can be downloaded and used.

www.readingpath.org — Caters to four main areas: Infants/Toddlers; Preschoolers; Kindergartners; and Grades 1-3. A service provided by the ERIC Clearinghouse on Elementary and Early Childhood Education.

www.readwritethink.org — *Provides educators and students access to the highest quality practices and resources in reading and language arts instruction.* The site features sections on *Learning Language, Learning About Language,* and *Learning Through Language.*

www.SavingTeachersMoney.com — A commercial site with discounts on numerous products for educators.

www.schooldiscovery.com/schrockguide — Kathy Schrock's Guide for Educators provides a list of web sites that are useful for curricula planning and professional development.

www.schoolnotes.com — Provides a wide variety of resources for students, teachers and parents. Enables teachers to post notes for homework and class information on the web, and for students and parents to view the information by entering their school ZIP code.

www.sdcoe.K12.ca.us/score/cla.html — Content materials and activities aligned to the Californian Content Standards. The site *includes Literature Guides, Language Arts Frameworks, Phonics Links,* and *Reading Initiatives.*

www.sitesforteachers.com	Contains over 650 sites in the database and claims to be, *the Net's best resource for teachers.*
www.skewlsites.com	*Provides a number of educational web sites.*
www.sparknotes.com	Contains a number of study guides for major works of literature.
www.teachernet.com	A major online source for K-8 educators with numerous resources and activities for the classroom.
www.teachersdesk.com	An educational resource containing lesson plans, advice, other useful links and discussion forums on various topics of interest.
www.teachingideas.com	A UK web site designed for teachers who teach primary children (ages 5-11).
www.teachersource@pbs.org	Provides over 2,500 lesson plans and activities in Arts & Literature, Health & Fitness, Mathematics, Science & Technology, Social Studies, and Early Childhood, for PreK – 12 educators.
www.teach-nology.com	Provides teachers with free access to 1000's of lesson plans, worksheets, web sites, rubrics, educational games, teaching tips, teaching advice, current news items, and other teaching tools.
www.theeducatorsnetwork.com	Provides a network of sites that include lesson plans, work sheets, theme units, teaching strategies, instructional materials, and educational resources.
www.thegateway.org	Provides, *high quality lesson plans, curricula units, and other educational resources,* located on government and commercial web sites.

www.uoregon.edu   PIZZAZ! Provides free, simple, creative writing
                  and oral storytelling activities for students of all ages.

http://vos.ucsb.edu/shuttle/eng-mod.html   A number of secondary and college resource
                  lists, *organized and maintained by scholars*.

www.youth.net   Aims to provide K-12 students and educators with
                  the opportunity to share their ideas and projects with
                  the global community.

NOTES

100

NOTES

ISBN 141200746-1

9 781412 007467